THE *Little Book* OF

~ RENOIR ~

A RICH AND VARIED
SELECTION OF RENOIR'S
BEST-KNOWN PAINTINGS

DEDICATION
For Russell

Editor: Fleur Robertson
Editorial Assistance: Kirsty Wheeler
Original Design Concept: Peter Bridgewater
Design: Stonecastle Graphics Ltd
Production Director: Gerald Hughes
Production: Ruth Arthur, Sally Connolly, Neil Randles
Typesetting: Julie Smith

CLB 3143
© 1993 Colour Library Books Ltd
Godalming, Surrey, England.
Printed and bound in Singapore.

ISBN 1 85833 079 3

THE *Little Book* OF

RENOIR

JULIET RODWAY

Colour Library Books

Introduction

Renoir's paintings are perhaps the most accessible and best loved of all the Impressionists' work. His pictures are first and foremost a celebration of the pleasures of life and as such they have an enduring appeal. In a career lasting nearly sixty years he painted on all subjects, from people at their leisure to bright landscapes, from sophisticated society portraits to innocent children. Finally, he devoted himself to portraying the delights of the female form in dozens of nudes. Rich, evocative and highly sensual, they fulfilled his desire to create paintings that are both beautiful and pleasurable.

Pierre-Auguste Renoir was born in Limoges on 25 February, 1841. Three years later the family moved to Paris, where Renoir's father, a tailor, hoped to improve his ailing business. The young boy showed early signs of artistic talent and at the age of thirteen he was apprenticed as a porcelain painter to the firm of Levy Brothers. Here he copied designs onto plates – often taken from paintings by French eighteenth-century masters – which instilled in him a lifelong passion for the work of Boucher, Fragonard and Watteau. When the porcelain factory closed down he earned his living decorating blinds and fans before eventually enrolling at Charles Gleyre's studio in Paris, where he studied art full time. His fellow students included Monet, Sisley and Bazille, who shared his ambitions to paint pictures of everyday life rather than the classical subjects advocated by the academic painters in vogue at the time. Monet, in particular, became a close friend and together, painting in the open air, they created some of the earliest Impressionist pictures.

In 1874 the Impressionists held their first 'Independent' exhibition. Besides Renoir and Monet, the leading contributors included Pissarro, Cézanne, Degas and Morisot. This important event was scorned by both the critics and the public, who condemned the artists for their sketchy technique, bright colours and contemporary subject matter. Unlike Monet, Renoir did not stick consistently to his Impressionist principles. As chiefly a figure painter, and after years of poverty and hardship, he frequently turned to conventional portraiture in order to make a living.

In the 1880s Renoir rejected his Impressionist style, feeling that he had exhausted all its possibilities. Instead, he looked to the 'art of the museums', and especially to Raphael and Ingres, to help him rediscover traditional themes and painting techniques. This, he felt, would create an art more durable than one based on the impressions of a fleeting moment. To many, the sharp linear style which resulted seemed out of character, and indeed it was only a matter of time before he reverted to his former relaxed manner.

In 1890, Renoir married his long-time mistress Aline Charigot. By now he was financially secure and he could be more selective over his commissions.

He spent the last thirty years of his life almost exclusively painting women and children – most notably a series of nudes, harking back to the works of Rubens and Titian as his role models.

Renoir once declared that he did not have 'the temperament of a fighter'. He was, however, to battle courageously against severe arthritis, which afflicted him from his late fifties right up until his death on 3 December, 1919. Always he continued to paint, strapping his brushes to his wrists when his hands were too crippled to hold them. In spite of the terrible pain, he still painted 'happy' pictures, without a trace of bitterness or pessimism. In 1910, writing to a young artist, he summed up his art's objectives, 'For me a picture ... should be something likeable, joyous and pretty – yes, pretty. There are enough ugly things in life for us not to add to them'. In Renoir's work we are taken to places where the sun shines and people smile, to a beautiful world made eternal through his art.

Mademoiselle Romaine Lacaux

Renoir's talent for portraiture clearly shines through in this captivating study of nine-year-old Romaine Lacaux. Although an early work, he has skilfully captured the girl's fragile beauty, delightfully combining it with an expression of youthful alertness. The natural grace and innocence of children genuinely enchanted Renoir; he never tired of painting them and in later life frequently used his own sons as models.

Completed shortly after Renoir left the Gleyre studio, this delicate painting is one of the few to have survived from the period 1862-66, as Renoir, displeased with his work during that time, is said to have destroyed most of it. The commission may have come through Renoir's contacts in the porcelain trade as Romaine's father was a manufacturer of terracotta goods.

1864
81 x 65 cm
Oil on canvas
The Cleveland Museum of Art, Ohio

The Sisleys

Renoir met the landscape painter Alfred Sisley, together with Monet and Bazille, at Charles Gleyre's studio in Paris where they were all students. The four artists worked in close association in these early days, often posing for each other's paintings and this was the case here. The woman is usually considered to be Sisley's wife, Eugénie, but she also bears a remarkable resemblance to Lise Tréhot, Renoir's model at this time.

The picture may have been painted in response to Monet's *Le Déjeuner sur l'herbe* and *Women in the Garden* of 1865-7, both of which dealt with figures in a landscape. However, whereas Monet, painting out of doors, was interested in the effects of light on the whole scene, Renoir was clearly more concerned with the figures themselves, and only hazily sketched in the background.

1868
106 x 74 cm
Oil on canvas
Wallraf-Richartz Museum, Cologne

La Grenouillère

La Grenouillère, literally The Frog Pool, was a popular recreational spot on the River Seine between Bougival and Chatou, just outside Paris. In the summer of 1869 Renoir and Monet painted there side by side in the open air, trying to capture the festival atmosphere in a succession of rapid sketches. This painting shows the narrow footbridge which connected the bank to a small, artificial island known as 'The Flowerpot'. Bold horizontal brushstrokes in unmixed colours suggest the play of light on the water, and deft vertical touches indicate the figures.

Originally intended as studies for more 'finished' studio-based pictures, these undeniably fresh sketches were later viewed by the artists as works of art in their own right. They are now considered to be some of the earliest 'impressionistic' works.

1869
65 x 93 cm
Oil on canvas
Oskar Reinhart Collection, Winterthur

The Odalisque

This alluring odalisque, or concubine, was based on Eugène Delacroix's sumptuous paintings of women in the harem. Renoir had a lifelong admiration for this great French artist, particularly revering his imaginative use of rich, warm colours and the intoxicating atmosphere in his pictures – Renoir swore he could smell the incense in them!

Although in 1870 the current fashion in Europe was for Japanese exotica (and had been since the 1850s), Renoir always preferred the orientalism of North Africa – no doubt it appealed to the sensual side of his nature. Draped in her richly patterned silk robes, this reclining woman gives Renoir the perfect opportunity to demonstrate his mastery of colour, as well as displaying the charms of his model and mistress Lise Tréhot.

1870
68 x 123 cm
Oil on canvas
National Gallery of Art, Washington D.C.

$\mathscr{P}$ath $\mathscr{T}$hrough $\mathscr{L}$ong $\mathscr{G}$rass

Renoir spent the summers of 1873 and 1874 with Monet and his family at Argenteuil, a small town on the Seine near Paris. Working together, often on identical subjects, they created some of their finest Impressionist pictures. By insisting they paint in the open air, Monet encouraged Renoir to lighten his colours and to use freer brushstrokes. This canvas is closely modelled on Monet's famous *Wild Poppies* of 1873, but was probably painted slightly later. Each picture shows two pairs of figures wandering gently down a grassy slope scattered with poppies.

Although Renoir considered himself primarily a figure painter, he valued the knowledge he gained from observing nature. Years later, towards the end of his life, he was to write, 'A painter can't be great if he doesn't understand landscape'.

c.1874
59 x 74 cm
Oil on canvas
Musée d'Orsay, Paris

La Loge

....

In the spring of 1874 Renoir took part in the first Impressionist Exhibition, showing six paintings including this striking portrait of a couple in a theatre box (*la loge* of the title). Renoir's younger brother, Edmond, posed alongside the beautiful and elegantly dressed artist's model Nini Lopez – most oddly nicknamed 'fish-face'!

Considering Renoir's love of women, it is not surprising that he chose to depict the attractions of his female sitter, rather than try to recreate the atmosphere on stage as Degas did in his theatre paintings. Although Renoir's approach may be more conventional, the composition does not lack individuality. At a time when many of the Impressionists were eliminating black from their palettes, Renoir used this 'queen of colours' to give his figures a powerful presence.

1874
80 x 63 cm
Oil on canvas
Courtauld Institute Galleries, London

Countryside under Snow

Unlike Monet, Sisley and Pissarro, Renoir painted few snowscapes. 'I have never been able to stand the cold', he told the dealer Ambroise Vollard. 'In any case ... why paint snow? It is one of nature's illnesses'. However, despite this belief, Renoir has succeeded here in painting one of his loveliest landscapes. It is similar in style to Monet's Argenteuil canvases of 1875, suggesting that Renoir was still under his friend's influence, at least as far as landscapes were concerned.

By studying nature closely the Impressionists had realised that the snow's surface takes on the colour of its surroundings. Here Renoir puts this observation into practice, delicately tinting the snow blue where it reflects the azure sky, and adding a rich, warm orange in the places touched by the glow of the wintry afternoon sun.

1875
51 x 66 cm
Oil on canvas
Musée de l'Orangerie, Paris

Victor Choquet

On 24 March, 1875, Renoir tried to raise money by organising an auction of Impressionist paintings in Paris. The sale turned into a disaster when angry demonstrators, outraged by the new style of painting, interrupted the proceedings.

One onlooker, though, was deeply impressed with the works of art on show. Victor Choquet, a customs official of modest means yet an avid art collector, fell in love with Impressionism that day. After the sale he commissioned Renoir to paint several portraits of his family and himself.

In this beautiful study Choquet is shown as a sensitive and intelligent man. Renoir rarely went beyond depicting the surface appearance of his sitters, but in this, probably his finest male portrait, he seems to have captured the very essence of this far-seeing, passionate art lover.

1876
47 x 37 cm
Oil on canvas
Fogg Art Museum, Cambridge, Mass.

The Swing

Following the sale of a large figure painting in 1875, Renoir was able to rent lodgings and a studio at 12 Rue Cortot, Montmartre. There, in the rather overgrown garden, he executed some of his most accomplished Impressionist paintings, including this one.

The relaxed mood of this canvas is typical of his work in the 1870s. Part of the painting's charm lies in Renoir's skilful rendering of the light filtering through the trees. However, when the canvas was shown in 1877 at the third Impressionist Exhibition, this technique met with much criticism. One writer complained that the sunlight effects looked like 'spots of grease on the models' clothes'!

The picture was bought by Renoir's friend, the wealthy painter and collector Gustave Caillebotte, who bequeathed it to the State in 1894.

1876
92 x 73 cm
Oil on canvas
Musée d'Orsay, Paris

Le Moulin de la Galette

It was once said of Renoir that he never produced a sad painting and indeed his undoubted *joie-de-vivre* is brilliantly reflected in this lively impression of a Parisian open-air dance hall.

With this ambitious canvas – one of his largest – Renoir aimed to create an authentic bohemian atmosphere. He persuaded some of the young working-class girls who frequented the Moulin to pose for him with a few of his painter friends. According to the writer Georges Rivière, who appears seated at the table, Renoir painted the canvas on the spot, carrying it daily from his studio nearby. With hardly a sharp edge anywhere, the work has a great sense of movement, perfectly capturing the spirit of this joyous occasion.

1876
131 x 175 cm
Oil on canvas
Musée d'Orsay, Paris

Madame Charpentier and her Children

To gain official recognition, and hopefully some commissions, Renoir abandoned the 1879 Impressionist show in favour of the Establishment-preferred art exhibition known as the Salon, where this triple portrait was accepted. The wife of an influential publisher, Madame Charpentier was renowned for her literary salons, which were attended by celebrities from the world of politics, literature and the arts. Her high social standing meant that the painting was well positioned at the exhibition, contributing greatly to its success.

Renoir had altered his technique to suit the conservative Salon, but was still censured for his lack of draughtsmanship. Although some Impressionists felt betrayed by Renoir's move, Pissarro, at least, did not begrudge his good fortune: he knew it was 'a hard life being poor'.

1878
154 x 190 cm
Oil on canvas
Metropolitan Museum of Art, New York

The Skiff

The Impressionists were fascinated by water and loved to paint the various leisure pursuits that took place on the River Seine. Between 1879 and 1880 Renoir painted several landscapes on a boating theme, but he rarely surpassed the intense luminosity he achieved in this sparkling picture.

The orange skiff forms a strong focal point, contrasting superbly with the deep blue of the water. However, the painting is really brought to life by the hundreds of tiny strokes of colour which Renoir used to show the river's rippling surface.

In later life Renoir looked back to these balmy days with great nostalgia. 'You could still enjoy yourself in those days. Machinery did not take up the whole of life'. Only the steam train in the distance interrupts the tranquillity of this scene.

1879
71 x 92 cm
Oil on canvas
The National Gallery, London

32

Luncheon of the Boating Party

This famous painting marks the high point of Renoir's Impressionist career. It is a brilliant portrayal of a relaxed summer gathering of his friends and is one of his last works based on the camaraderie of his early life.

The setting is the terrace of Alphonse Fournaise's restaurant at Chatou – a popular meeting place with the rowers who liked this part of the Seine. The painter and collector Gustave Caillebotte, a keen oarsman, can be seen seated to the right, and the young woman holding the dog is Aline Charigot, Renoir's future wife. Love is in the air everywhere in this picture – virtually everyone in the painting appears to be flirting with someone else, either in conversation or by making eye contact. Perhaps, therefore, it is right that Renoir's beloved only looks adoringly at her dog.

1880-1
130 x 173 cm
Oil on canvas
Phillips Collection, Washington D.C.

St Mark's Square, Venice

At the beginning of 1881 Renoir started to sell his paintings on a regular basis to the dealer Paul Durand-Ruel, a loyal supporter of the Impressionists. The improvement in his finances gave him the freedom to travel widely, especially in North Africa and Europe. In October, 1881, he visited Italy with the intention of studying Classical and Renaissance art. Whilst in Venice he sketched the city's famous landmarks, later reworking those canvases he hoped to sell. He was particularly taken with St Mark's Basilica: 'What a welcome change from all those cold Renaissance churches ... one immediately feels one has entered a very holy place because of this spiritual atmosphere'.

This study, which he did not retouch, has an ethereal, early morning quality reminiscent of Turner's famous paintings of Venice.

1881
65 x 81 cm
Oil on canvas
The Minneapolis Institute of Arts

Fruits du Midi

Still life formed a significant part of Renoir's repertoire. When his figure paintings failed to sell still lifes proved a more reliable source of income. Like many other artists, Renoir found painting still lifes a useful means of improving his technique without fear of wasting a model's time or ruining the picture. This relaxed approach resulted in some of his most beautiful canvases: these succulent Mediterranean fruits convey the same feeling of sensuality as his most voluptuous nudes. Indeed, Renoir once said that he painted figures 'as if they were some splendid fruit'.

In later life he produced many small canvases which varied enormously in quality. In 1901, he grumpily told the dealer Durand-Ruel (who bought large numbers of his still lifes over the years), 'if I only sold good things, I would die of hunger'.

1881
51 x 69 cm
Oil on canvas
The Art Institute of Chicago

Dance in the Country

Between 1882 and 1883 Renoir worked on three almost life-size canvases on the theme of dancing couples. Two, *Dance in the Country* and *Dance in the City*, were painted as a pair. In the latter, Renoir depicted the couple in elegant surroundings and formal dress, contrasting clearly with the more relaxed occasion shown here. The models in this instance were the journalist Paul Lhote and Renoir's voluptuous mistress, Aline Charigot.

Although the colour and subject matter of this painting are typical of Renoir's Impressionist work, he no longer filled the canvas to overflowing with people or merged the figures with the background as in *Le Moulin de la Galette*. Instead, a simple discarded hat and the half-finished meal at the table are enough to suggest the carefree atmosphere of this informal suburban cabaret.

1882-3
180 x 90 cm
Oil on canvas
Musée d'Orsay, Paris

$\mathcal{U}mbrellas$

The wonderful rhythmical arrangement of the umbrellas transforms a potentially dreary subject into this lively evocation of modern life. It also links either side of the picture, which Renoir painted at different dates and in contrasting styles.

The figures to the right, begun in 1881, are painted with the soft, feathery brushstrokes and luminous colours of Renoir's Impressionist period. The woman to the left, however, and the umbrellas and figures beyond, are drawn more sharply, suggesting they were painted later – probably around 1885 judging from the difference in the women's fashions. By then Renoir, unhappy with Impressionism and its concentration on a brief moment, had returned to more traditional painting methods based on a greater use of outline.

1881-5
180 x 115 cm
Oil on canvas
The National Gallery, London

$\mathcal{C}$ountryside around $\mathcal{M}$enton

In December, 1883, Renoir spent two weeks painting on the French Mediterranean coast between Marseille and Genoa. At Menton and all along the Riviera, he was dazzled by the subtle variations of colour in the landscape, and he struggled to capture them to his satisfaction on canvas. His success is evident in this painting.

After 1898 Renoir regularly returned to the south, particularly to Cagnes, just west of Nice, where he loved to paint the olive groves on the hillside estate of Les Collettes – although not always without difficulty. 'The olive tree, what a brute! ... Its little leaves, how they've made me sweat!' When a timber merchant threatened to buy the estate and fell the olive trees, Renoir, with some encouragement from Aline, purchased it and in 1907 it became his permanent home.

1883
66 x 81 cm
Oil on canvas
Museum of Fine Arts, Boston

Madame Clapisson

This charming, conventionally posed study was Renoir's second attempt at painting Madame Clapisson. The first canvas, a full-length portrait painted in light tones and showing her seated on a garden bench surrounded by brightly coloured flowers, was rejected by the Clapissons as too daring. Renoir was asked to produce another picture in more muted tones. Even so, he did not conform entirely to traditional portrait practices. Instead of painting in the usual dark background, he chose to enliven the surface with vigorous brushstrokes in a subtle combination of red, blue and yellow tints, reserving the more delicate brushwork for the sitter's porcelain skin. The portrait was Renoir's only entry in the 1883 Salon. He sold the earlier canvas (once he had concealed the model's identity) to a buyer in New York.

1883
82 x 65 cm
Oil on canvas
The Art Institute of Chicago

The Bathers

The Bathers was the most ambitious painting executed during Renoir's experimental phase. In subject matter and in style, it could not be further removed from his Impressionist works.

Rather than paint a scene from everyday life, Renoir chose the classic theme of the female nude in a landscape, which he had come to regard as one of the 'most essential forms of art'. By clearly defining the figures, and by making no attempt to render effects of light or to suggest a particular historical moment, Renoir gives the scene a feeling of timelessness. Unfortunately, few of his friends appreciated the change in style, neither liking nor understanding it. After 1888 Renoir returned to his familiar feathery brushstrokes, but he never completely reverted to his Impressionist concerns.

1887
115 x 170 cm
Oil on canvas
Philadelphia Museum of Art

Young Girls at the Piano

In 1892 Renoir was commissioned by the French State to produce a major new painting to be hung in the prestigious Luxembourg Palace, a museum devoted to the work of living artists.

Keen to make a good impression, Renoir painted six versions – one pastel and five oils – of his *Young Girls at the Piano*, leaving the final selection to Henri Roujon, the French Minister of Fine Arts. Somewhat spoilt for choice, the Minister eventually decided on the picture shown opposite. Later, Renoir felt that the State's purchase, for which he had received 4,000 francs, was not necessarily the best. Yet despite Renoir's reservations, the painting was considered a success when it was first shown. As a result of the State's recognition, his works became more fashionable and demand for them increased, securing the artist's financial future.

1892
116 x 90 cm
Oil on canvas
Musée d'Orsay, Paris

La Dormeuse

Nothing could better illustrate Renoir's highly sensual approach to art than the nudes he painted in his last thirty years, of which *La Dormeuse* (*The Sleeper*) is a fine example. Although she reclines in a provocative pose, this sleeping beauty is gently seductive rather than overtly erotic.

Renoir rarely portrayed the personal characteristics of his models, especially of his nudes. Instead he tended to make them all alike to conform to his idea of female perfection — a rounded figure, small nose, girlish features, soft radiant skin, and luscious ruby red lips. Renoir preferred his women to be sweet, simple beings, child-like and without pretensions. He is even said to have encouraged trite conversations with his models in order to evoke the dreamy facial expression which typifies the 'Renoir woman'.

1897
80 x 62 cm
Oil on canvas
Oskar Reinhart Collection, Winterthur

Gabrielle and Jean

In spite of the serene atmosphere in his paintings, Renoir was a somewhat restless, anxious man. His marriage to Aline in 1890, five years after the birth of Pierre (the first of their three sons), brought him a measure of stability and domestic bliss.

When Jean was born in 1894 Aline's cousin, Gabrielle Renard, was hired as a nursemaid. Over the next twenty years she posed for Renoir on countless occasions – either on her own or, as here, helping to amuse the children. Renoir demanded of his servants only that their skin 'took the light' well. It is not surprising that Gabrielle's luminous young skin usually proved a more attractive proposition for portrait painting than Madame Renoir's. Aline was by 1900 nearing forty and had become extremely overweight.

1900
65 x 54 cm
Oil on canvas
Musée de l'Orangerie, Paris

54

Ambroise Vollard

This painting of the art dealer Ambroise Vollard is one of the few male portraits Renoir painted after 1890. Vollard's gallery on the rue Lafitte was a major outlet for Renoir's work during the last twenty years of his career, making Vollard a client worthy of being made an exception to the rule.

The dealer is shown holding a statuette by the sculptor Maillol, who had been commissioned by Vollard to make a bust of Renoir around the same date as this portrait. Later, when Renoir found it hard to paint, crippled as he was by arthritis, Vollard suggested that he take up sculpture. However, the painter's hands were so deformed and unresponsive that this was a difficult task. The problem was solved by employing assistants who modelled the clay under Renoir's direction – usually given with the aid of a long stick!

1908
82 x 64 cm
Oil on canvas
Courtauld Institute Galleries, London

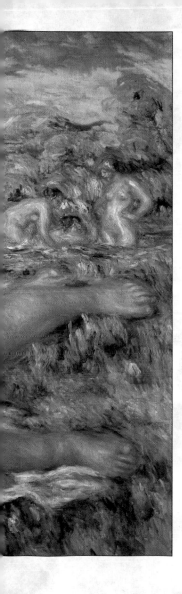

Bathing Women

In this timeless vision of the female nude, Renoir recalls *The Bathers* of 1887. Yet the soft, caressing brushstrokes used here are in marked contrast to the crisp outlines of the earlier painting.

Renoir considered this large-scale canvas his final masterpiece and did not rest until he had completed it. Ill health confined him to a wheelchair, so he could only reach the top of the painting by means of an adjustable easel that allowed him to roll the canvas up or down. Despite his great age and physical disabilities, Renoir was ever seeking to breathe new life into traditional subjects. 'I'm trying to fuse the landscape with my figures', he said in 1918, 'the old masters never attempted this'. Determined and brave to the end, Renoir, in this last great painting, achieved his aim.

1918-19
110 x 160 cm
Oil on canvas
Musée d'Orsay, Paris

$\mathcal{A}cknowledgements$

The publishers would like to thank the following for
permission to reproduce:–

A. K.G., Berlin, for pp. 13, 16-17, 36-37, 53;

Art Resource, New York, with acknowledgements to
Giraudon, Paris, for the back flap
and pp. 11, 18, 26, 28-29, 41, 50, 55, 58-59;

The Bridgeman Art Library, London, for the jacket,
the title page, the last page and pp. 14-15, 21,
22-23 and with acknowledgements to Giraudon,
Paris, for pp. 25, 30, 32-33, 34-35, 43, 48-49;

Picturepoint, Windsor,
for pp. 38-39, 44-45, 47, 56.

Title page and facing page:
Leontine and Coco
Private collection